Samuel Arnold, John Scawen

New Spain or Love in Mexico

An opera in three acts

Samuel Arnold, John Scawen

New Spain or Love in Mexico
An opera in three acts

ISBN/EAN: 9783741144257

Manufactured in Europe, USA, Canada, Australia, Japa

Cover: Foto ©Andreas Hilbeck / pixelio.de

Manufactured and distributed by brebook publishing software
(www.brebook.com)

Samuel Arnold, John Scawen

New Spain or Love in Mexico

NEW SPAIN,

OR,

LOVE IN MEXICO:

AN

O P E R A,

IN THREE ACTS;

AS PERFORMED AT THE

THEATRE - ROYAL

IN THE

HAY-MARKET.

First Acted on Friday, July 16, 1790.

———————

LONDON:

PRINTED FOR G. G. J. AND J. ROBINSON, PATER-
NOSTER-ROW.

————

M.DCC.XC.

DRAMATIS PERSONÆ.

Don Lopez, - - -	Mr. RYDER.
Don Garcias, - -	Mr. WATERHOUSE.
Don Juan, - - -	Mr. DAVIES.
Alkmonoak - -	Mr. BANNISTER.
Zempoalla - - -	Mr. CUBIT.
Fabio - - - -	Mr. J. BANNISTER.
Secretary to Don Lopez, -	Mr. R. PALMER.
Servant, - -	Mr. LEDGER.

WOMEN.

Leonora, - - -	Mrs. GOODALL.
Julia, - - - -	Mrs. ILIFF.
Ifcagli, - . -	Mrs. BANNISTER.
Flora, - - - -	Miſs FONTENELLE.
Ulah, - - -	Mrs. EDWARDS.
Caduga, - -	Miſs PALMER.

Council——Soldiers——Indians.

(The Parts marked by inverted Commas are omitted in the
Reprefentation.)

NEW SPAIN:

OR,

LOVE in MEXICO.

AN

OPERA.

ACT I.

SCENE I.

The Ramparts of a Spanish *Town in* New Mexico.

Enter Leonora *and* Flora *drest as men in military habits and cloaks;* (Leonora, *richly habited, with an order)* *and an escort of soldiers.*

Flora. I BESEECH your Excellency let us to bed again—these abominable rounds !—Serjeant, you are dismiss'd——   [*Exit Escort.*

Leonora. Hark ye, Lieutenant, this unmilitary disposition stands in the way of your preferment :—the whole garrison murmured when I made you my Aid de Camp.

Flora. Your Excellency should really make some allowance for a certain delicacy of frame, and the habits

B   of

of paſt life, and *(looks around and half whispers)* a ſex not abſolutely accuſtomed to——

Leonora. Well fellow ! and what am I ?

Flora. Fellow ! Upon my life, Madam—Sir, I mean—

Leonora. Be more diſcreet for heaven's ſake— how do I bear all this ?

Flora. Habit and inclination, Colonel ; why I have heard the old Count, your father, ſay that, even in the nurſery, you beat your brother at his own weapons ; and I am ſure all Valentia talk'd of your horſemanſhip. Why, Madam, did not the ſlave Sadi, the treacherous confidant of the too credulous Don Garcias——

Leonora. Credulous indeed ! his credulity has prov'd fatal to us all !

Flora. Did not that villainous Moor, when he had ſeduced us on board the Barbary zebecque, under pretence of conducting us to your lover, Don Garcias—did not he then, confeſs to me that your fondneſs for the maſculine exerciſes firſt ſuggeſted to him the idea of facilitating our eſcape by means of our preſent diſguiſes ?

Leonora. Name the wretch no more.

Flora. And, Madam, after we had been ſo luckily reſcued by the Spaniſh man of war, and when we were taken up, as ſhe was upon the point of foundering, by the veſſel which convey'd the Viceroy hither to New Mexico— did not your Ladyſhip's manly conduct, during a ſevere engagement, ſo far recommend you to his eſteem as to procure for you your preſent exalted poſt ?

Leonora. In which I have paſſed two whole years without detection.

Flora. True, Madam, and yet you had a narrow eſcape, when the old Governor, in conſequence of

your

your favour with the Viceroy, was so anxious that you shou'd marry his daughter, Donna Julia.

Leonora. To that event I am indebted for the sweetest alleviation which a destiny like mine can know; by making a confidant of Donna Julia I have effectually secur'd my secret, and gain'd the most charming, the most faithful of friend—but—to the news you brought me this morning—is it certain?

Flora. Certain!—Sir, you are my commanding officer, and Lieutenant-Governor of this place—yet give me leave to tell you, Sir, my Honour——

Leonora. Leave this folly and proceed.

Flora. When your Excellency sent me last night with orders to the officer on guard at the Western Gate, I saw four persons enter the town.

Leonora. One of whom was——

Flora. Patience, Sir,—Consider, 'tis a manly virtue.

Leonora. Go on——

Flora. One of whom was——

Leonora. Garcias?

Flora. An Indian Chief—He was attended by two Spanish officers and a servant—one of those officers resembled Don Garcias, but his man I will swear was his old servant Fabio, and my quondam lover.

Leonora. Ah Flora! *(sighing).*

Flora. Hush! hush! Good Colonel, who is indiscreet now?

Leonora. Garcias here!—Ah silly bosom, dost thou already swell with a hope so slightly founded?

Flora. Somebody comes this way—whoever he is, he is an early walker—let us retire: your Honour knows there may be danger to the fort—if he shou'd prove a certain stranger! *(they retire).*

Enter

Enter Fabio.

Fabio. No bed to-night neither !——What with fighting, watching, prifons, and efcapes—I believe I fhall never lie down again—Oh ! for the gentlemanly luxury of a feather-bed—to repofe on the fpoils of a few hundred geefe, all contributing to my fupport !— there is fome ftate in that——'tis the way all great men reft——

Flora. (afide.) How the puppy moralifes—Prifons and efcapes though betray but a fufpicious kind of knowledge ; I fhall make bold to queftion this fellow.

Fabio. Oh ! for a bed of down *(yawns)*—down ! down ! derry down !

Flora. I wifh your Excellency had not difmiffed the guard.

Leonora, Surely the great Sebaftian cannot fear ! ——Two of us to a man unarmed !——

Flora. Ambufcades Sir !—that's my dread, they make fuch an ugly ftory——however, to my duty. *(She draws near and fteals round.)* Stand, you dog, you are my prifoner.

*(*Fabio *attempts to run off and is ftopped by* Leonora.)*

Leonora. Who are you, fellow ? and what do you on the ramparts ?

Fabio. I do nothing on the ramparts—as you fee gentlemen.

Flora (afide), Your fervant, Mr Fabio.——I recollect this fellow now—did not you come into town laft night with two officers, and an Indian Chief?

Fabio. I did, Sir, to my misfortune.

Flora. Leave prating fellow, Don Garcias is one of them.

Fabio. Yes, Sir—I am his humble—his confidential friend—and fervant.

Flora.

Flora. I told your Excellency I was right—we have the bird in the cage.

Fabio. Oh! the devil! what have I said?

Leonora (with hesitation). Don Garcias?

Fabio. Ye---es, Sir.

Leonora (with increasing hesitation). Of Valentia, perhaps?

Fabio. Valentia! Lord,—no, Sir—my master comes from——plague on it—'tis a place of two, two or three syllables—and begins with a vowel.

Flora. Guadalaxara?

Fabio. The same, the same—plague on my stupid head.—Yes Don Garcias of Guadalaxara.

Flora. A name of two or three syllables, and beginning with a vowel.

Fabio. Whether two, three, or four syllables, I could not tell. But I was sure it began with either a vowel, or a consonant.

Flora. You were?—Friend, if your master has as much wit as his man, he may be worth seeing—I wish your Excellency wou'd send for him—I have a reason for it.

Leonora. I wish to see Don Garcias—present the Lieutenant-Governor's respects, and tell him so.

Fabio. Ye---es, my Lord, I shall signify your commands with the profoundest——

Flora. Cease chattering, fellow, and deliver your message.   [*Exit Fabio.*

Leonora. Now, Flora, what is your intelligence worth? Let me tell you—this folly does not meet with my warmest approbation.

Flora. My life on it, Madam, I am right yet.—I know that chattering fellow as well as I know the cut of your Ladyship's small cloaths—what tho' his whisker is a little thicker—and his face a little browner, and his shoulder a little broader.

Leonora.

Leonora. Do you mention all this to convince me that you know him?

Flora. Then his tongue—I'd swear to his tongue —and yet if I did I should swear to a *false thing*—for he has so lyed to me!

Leonora. Follow him however, if his master should prove the true Garcias he may attempt his escape.

Flora. I'll give the necessary orders at the gate, in the mean time, Madam, be comforted—I'll stake my honour—as a soldier, I mean—that my assertions are well founded.

Leonora. Heaven grant it may prove so—meet me at home soon as you have given your orders. [*Exit Flora.*] I will seek my Julia of whose soothing friendship I have at present so much need.—Fate may perhaps relent and smile at length on that love which its malice hath tried in vain to subdue.

S O N G.

With many a sed intrusive doubt opprest,
   As the pale maiden eyes her plighted youth,
While threat'ning absence chills her glowing breast,
   Let pitying love inspire this holy truth.

Though trackless climes to part them interfere,
   Still heart to heart shall beat, as fondly true
As when blest bosoms, that sole barrier
   Which mutual pressures labour to subdue.

                       [Exit.

SCENE

SCENE II.

Enter Alkmonoak *and* Don Garcias.

Alkm. Thanks to the brightness of the morning, I have almost lost the remembrance of my late danger—I hope we may now exchange congratulations on our mutual safety.

Garcias. That you are safe, thank Heaven! but for me! hear the sad remainder of my story, and judge——

The father of this once unspotted beauty, this Leonora de Cespedes, favoured the pretensions of my wealthy rival, and she consented to elope with me. I sent a Moorish slave who had gain'd my confidence to conduct her to the spot where I waited with a vessel destined to convey us to Italy.—I waited in vain, the miserable girl disappear'd, nor was my slave heard of afterwards.

Alkm. Ignoble girl.

Garcias. " Circumstances established the probability of her having elop'd with me;" her family cited me to the provincial tribunal that I might produce her, and I was compell'd to fly from Valentia, " where I was in hourly danger of being apprehended as her murderer.—Gracious Heavens, the murderer of the woman I adored!"—The process of their courts has pursued me even hither, and I am now on my road to an English colony—in which, torn as my mind is, I seek at best but a comfortless asylum.

Alkm. From my soul I pity you.

Garcias. Good Heavens! how did I survive that fatal night, the solitary hours of which I counted on the sandy beach.—" I hailed the flapping of the idle sail, as a sound propitious to love and liberty, how dreadfully was I deceiv'd!"

SONG

S O N G.

Now Cynthia rode in silver car,
  The Heavens were clad in milder blue,
Now silence watch'd the winking star,
  With secrecy to lovers true.
The stately bark at anchor seem'd to sleep
On the slow-swelling bosom of the deep.

His tresses streaming to the breeze,
  Where hangs the sea-boy o'er the bow,
Who loves to loll in listless ease,
  And hear the wild wave talk below.
Or starts perchance to view the pendent sail
As, flapping loud, it chides th' intruding gale.

My fair one's faithful step to hear,
  I pause upon the grey sand's slope,
Each tardy hour sees icy fear
  Invade the glow of sick'ning hope.
'Till the sad dawn of unpropitious day
Beholds the bosom's last fond doubt decay.

Enter Don Juan.

Juan. What Garcias! for ever in this melancholy strain? My brave Chief, let me again congratulate you on your escape.——Little did I think, when your sudden approach alarmed us in the wood, that I was about to fire on the man, who had once sav'd my life.——

Alkm. No more of that—" the situation in which we met justified your apprehensions,"—to rush on you so, was imprudent, " but I fled from horrors to which common danger appeared a trifle."

                                        Garcias.

Garcias. Your escape seems miraculous.

Alkm. The ravage of fire, and the stupor of intoxication befriended me—the Indians who took me had been trafficing with some of your people for spirits, and I easily escaped from a guard, overcome at once with drunkenness and terror.

Juan. What cou'd have mov'd your enemy Zempoalla, to such acts of diabolical vengeance ?

Alkm. "The fate of war gave him the right, and the jealousy of a lover the will.—I was taken by him on a hunting party." I had formerly taken from him a female of uncommon beauty whom I have long lost; and lost I fear for ever.—Yet I will not complain— Fate surely relented when he bade me cross the path of my friends——

Juan. We were on our way hither from a neighbouring town.—Don Garcias proposes to retire to an English settlement, and I have been induc'd to accompany him thus far.——

Garcias (smiling). By my love for the fair Julia, the Governor's daughter.—Have not I concluded your speech properly ?

Juan. To be honest, you have.—Julia deign'd to smile on my humble love—but Don Lopez insisted on the exclusive privilege of a father, and formed for her a complete system of happiness to which she was the only person not admitted a party—his first step was to send me on that expedition in which I became your prisoner.—How nobly I was us'd; how the hand of friendship was extended to me when I expected the grasp of torture.——

Alkm. No more.—Torture, tho' often the test of fortitude, is the offspring of inhuman ferocity.—I was long a captive among Europeans—they taught me urbanity—but alas! their urbanity knew not integrity

C   —they

—they fmiled on me while they robb'd my heart of
its only treafure—my lov'd! my loft Ifcagli.

S O N G.

I have loft her; full weary is my heart,
Yet feeks in vain an object of repofe,
I have loft her; the fun which faw us part
Shall never fee the period of my woes.
Time ftrives in vain to bid my forrows reft
Or fill the cheerlefs void within my breaft.

Juan. Hark! fome perfon is coming this way—
as we are neither of us very anxious to be feen we
had better retire.—By the ftatelinefs of the ftep it
fhould be the Governor at leaft.   [*they retire.*

Enter Fabio.

Fabio. Where the devil is my wife mafter?——
Wandering fomewhere, I fuppofe, minding any thing
but his own bufinefs.—But I have a bolus for him—
difcover'd! (*makes figns of hanging*) never born to die
in his bed!—ah filly, filly,—filly Don Garcias.

Garcias (bowing). At your fervice, Sir: I am
forry to have interrupted fo pleafant a contemplation.

Fabio. I was indeed, Sir, lamenting thofe infir-
mities, which the greateft minds labour under.

Garcias. In fo often bringing the greateft bodies
into jeopardy—as for inftance, rafcal.——

Juan. Refpite the dog for a moment—there is
fomething ferious in this—did not you fay that your
mafter was difcover'd?

Fabio.

Fabio. I was feeking my mafter, Sir, with a meffage from the Lieutenant-Governor, who defires to fee him.

Garcias. You have betray'd me, firrah!

Fabio. Lord, Sir, you wou'd have betray'd yourfelf if you had been attacked by two ruffians as I was, devilifh ftout black wacking fellows with whifkers! Lord a mercy, they had terrible killing looks.

Garcias. Why fhould you mention my name, rafcal!

Fabio. Lord, Sir, there is no harm done.—I brought you off.—Let me alone for prefence of mind in the hour of danger.

Juan. How?

Fabio. Why, Sir, when the talleft of the two— but not quite fo horrible a looking dog as the other, faid in a gruff voice—is your mafter of Valentia?—

Garcias. You anfwer'd—

Fabio. No. Full mouthed.—Lord, Sir,—faid I, his worfhip is of Guadalaxara.

Juan. I have it—it is the Lieutenant-Governor who wifhes to fee your mafter?

Fabio. Yes, Sir.

Juan. I will go to him and affume your name Don Garcias—fhould any one here be, by chance, acquainted with your perfon, this and the province of Guadalaxara will effectually baffle them.

Garcias. May it not involve you in fome trouble?

Juan. Impoffible—he does not know me for he has been appointed fince my abfence.—I muft beg the affiftance of Fabio.

Garcias. Attend Don Juan, rafcal.

Fabio. Rafcal!—Sir, Don Garcias (*pointing to Juan*) may take thefe liberties with me—but give me leave to tell you—I am only a rafcal to my mafter.

[*Exit Fabio.*

Juan.

Juan. Garcias, Farewel—and prithee do not become so perfect a monopolizer of gloom and vapours; recollect that the Chief and I have a right to our share in these kind of follies as lovers.

Alkm. True; and I do not believe that love has three more zealous votaries than we are.

T R I O.

Three pilgrims, at love's sacred shrine we bow,
And breathe with holy zeal the fervent vow,
Mark'd by the mein enwrapt, the sigh of fire,
Senses subdu'd, and purified desire,
Nor meanly guerdon'd who shall these attain
By musing on the Heaven, they seek perhaps in vain.

[Exeunt.

S C E N E III.

The Hall of Audience in the Governor's Palace. Don Lopez *(the Governor) in Council,* Secretary, Zempoalla, *Guards, &c.*

Don Lopez. Come, Secretary, dispatch.

Secretary. I must transmit your Excellency's answer to the Chief of the Flat-headed Indians, who made his speech at the last audience.

Don Lopez. Good!—What was the speech about?

Secretary. A speech of thanks for our late assistance, couch'd in the sublime expressions of these people; it concluded that the tyger of desolation was about to ravage their country—when the generous " Lion," meaning your Lordship the Governor.—

I

Don Lopez.

Don Lopez. I recollect it now—it was prettily said, I will answer it—where is the Interpreter——— First, tell him, I am the Lion he talk'd of in his last speech.

Secretary. With submission, my Lord, he knows that before———But the Interpreter's suddenly taken ill.

Don Lopez. Is he ?—Then let my gracious answer be written down. If he can't get it tranflated when he gets home it will be the more valuable—No writings so esteemed as those which are not under-stood. Tell him the Flat-heads are very kind and civil and all that ; that it is very polite in them to confider me as a Lion, and very much according to the character of the Flat-heads in general, whom I shall henceforth look upon as my brethren.

Enter Zempoalla.

Secretary. My Lord, the Chief Zempoalla is come to prefer his final claim to the Indian Lady Iscagli, whom he says you detain from him.

Don Lopez. Ha ! has he not had my answer ?

Zempoalla. Lord Governor, I claim her as my Countrywoman.

Don Lopez (rising in passion). Break up the council.

Zempoalla. My Lord !———

Secretary (goes to him and claps his hand on his mouth). (Aside to Zempoalla). Watch the Governor out, and come to me in half an hour.   [*Exit* Zempoalla.

Enter Servant.

Servant. My Lord, the messenger is returned from the Indian Lady at the pavilion.

Don Lopez.

Don Lopez. I come. [*Exit Servant.*] Now for some news of my dear little Iscagli.—'Tis a pretty little tit—what a pair of eyes she has—they are never out of my sight—they perplex my very decrees; when I was ask'd the other day in council, what I would give as a subsidy to the Chief of the Chactaws, I answered with a sigh—Two such black eyes. Break up the council—Gentlemen to your several departments—that of sound and deep reflection on the public welfare, be mine.

[*The Council and Guards* Exeunt.

Don Lopez *and* Secretary *remain.*

Secretary. Well, my old dad that is to be, now ceremony is over, tip us your daddle.

Don Lopez (withdrawing his hand). Ha!—why, who am I, you dog? do you know me?

Secretary. Do you know me, if you come to that? Am not I a Commissary?——Did you ever know a Governor refuse to shake hands with a Commissary—'tis too ridiculous——

Don Lopez. Am not I an Hidalgo from the Mountains of Arragon, and an old Christian?

Secretary. And is not a Commissary a Christian too?

Don Lopez. Scarcely so—I think.

Secretary. Poh! Poh! this is carrying the jest a little too far——we are alone you know—why, friend Lopez, you are as distant as if I was one of your paltry nobility.

Don Lopez. Why, thou salter down of Old Bullocks——

Secretary. The older they are the fitter to die.—

Don Lopez. And for thy poison libelled by the harmless denomination of rum.——

Secretary.

Secretary. You cannot fay that's old, I'm fure.

Don Lopez. No—by St. Anthony, 'tis new enough to do its duty—Grape-fhot is a fool to it—thou exterminator of thy fellow-creatures!

Secretary. All heroes have been fo.

Don Lopez. For flaughter in the tented field; commend me to a bit of paper call'd a Victualling Contract—the fword of Alexander himfelf was but a conftable's ftaff to it.—That ever Don Lopez Antonio Perez de Valcabro de Redio de Montralva de Vega, fhou'd think of marrying his daughter to a retailer of rancid pork.

Secretary. Then you won't fhake hands?—There's a new contract.

Don Lopez. Vanifh mifcreant, or I'll break your bones.

Secretary. But one word more—*(goes up to his ear)* Snacks!

Don Lopez. Ah! you comical dog—you have fuch a winning way with you——but ftill I'll break your bones if you don't dine with me to-day.

DUETT.

Lop. { *Off you dog, or I'll crack your crown,*
{ *Hence from my fight!—away!—go!*

Sec.   *Snacks.*

Lop. *Zounds! what's become of all my wrath?*
Sure I'm as weak as barley broth.
What the devil makes me thus relax?

Sec.   *Why Snacks—Snacks!—Snacks.*

Lop. *When two rogues fquabble for a poor man's pelf,*
What puts an end to the ftrife?

Sec.   *Why Snacks.*

                            Lopez.

Lop.   *Both shake hands and forget to hate,*
         But fit coolly down and divide the estate.
         What makes knaves stick together like wax ?
Sec.   *Why Snacks ! Snacks ! Snacks.*
Lop.   *What makes the General fit him down,*
         Blind to the Commissary's tricks ?
Sec.   *Why Snacks.*
Lop.   *When the rascal's poison through the line runs,*
         More fatal and sure than the enemy's guns,
         Should the noose be deserves be tied, what lacks ?
Sec.   *Why Snacks !—Snacks ! Snacks !*

(Both shake hands heartily. *Exeunt* Sec. *and* Lopez.)

S C E N E   IV.   *A Garden.*

Enter Fabio *meeting* Flora.

Fabio.   Your most obedient and very devoted servant, Sir.

Flora.   Is Signor Don Garcias here ?

Fabio.   He is somewhere in the garden, Sir, waiting for the Lieutenant-Governor—pray, Sir, may I
venture to ask in what situation you have the honour
to attend his Excellency ?

Flora.   His Excellency has chosen me his Aid de
Camp ; doing me the honour to think that there is
something very similar in the ——

Fabio.   Colour of your beards, I presume.

Flora.   Why, Sir, the truth is, as you see, that
my promotion has been of quicker growth than my
whiskers.

S O N G.

SONG. Flora.

As the soldier's lad with his foraging cap
On the baggage rides in his mother's lap,
The captain eyes him with a father's joy,
And soon to a fife promotes the boy :
Now his sabre behind him he swings with an air,
And his ears are well flower'd, well pasted his hair ;
While his tassel'd hat with its weight crouds down
His chubby little face to a soldier's frown.

With a martial swagger loose he throws about
The natty (no) skirt of a quick-cut-coat ;
Mills a foul on the march for a gill of rum,
And his major pronounces him fit for a drum :
With his arms a-kimbo, then, the knowing young elf,
And a drum at his back twice as big as himself,
Sucks his teeth with an air, swears he'll make good his
*   quarters——*
So he does as he swears, with his landlady's daughters.

Can promotion be refus'd to talents so well suiting ?
He's a serjeant well fed, now, and fam'd for recruiting ;
Beneath sash and hat what a military grace,
For round is his belly, and red is his face :
Like a serjeant he swears, if he kicks but a straw,
And lyes like a serjeant—a serjeant at law ;
Yet serjeant or drum, shew a female or foe,
And you'll find him a soldier from top to toe.

Fabio. Well done my little Bantum Cock of the Camp.

Flora. You are witty, Sir.

Fabio. Yes, Sir, a man of—wit and pleasure, Sir.

Flora (aside). Ah! Villainous coxcomb, I'll

D   pump

pump the rogue.——A man of your figure has not
been without his gallantries.

Fabio. Oh no! What is life without love; and
what is love, my dear Sir, without variety.

Flora (aside). Yes, Yes, I see the villain—You
may by chance have been at Valentia.

Fabio. Valentia! O yes! yes!—No—no I mean,
that is, I myself have been there—but my master,
Don Garcias, never.

Flora. Never?

Fabio. Never, upon my honour.

Flora (coxcomically). I have heard that it is a fa-
mous place for intrigue.

Fabio. Has not its equal in all Spain, Sir. I myself was immerged in intrigue there.

Flora. Oh! you were?

Fabio. O yes, up to the eyes: they us'd to call
me Flint—cruel, hard-hearted, remorseless—an asper-
sion—I could not return the love of all, and so got
libell'd.

Flora. Flint!

Fabio. Yes, Flint.

Flora. I was quarter'd in Valentia once, and interested myself a good deal about one Flora de
Gambados.

Fabio. Ha! ha! ha!

Flora. Did you know her?

Fabio. Interested yourself—that's too good.

Flora. A good looking girl, I think——

Fabio. You are easily pleas'd, Sir.

Flora. Well—I was a good deal attached to her.

Fabio. I myself was slightly attached to her once
—but she grew so fond, I was obliged to fly for it—
truth is—I did promise the poor devil, marriage.

Flora. False Vill——I beg your pardon, Sir—but
perjury is nothing with you men of gallantry.

                                    Fabio.

Fabio. Nothing!—no, to be sure——If perjuries in love were punishable by the pillory, 'twould cause a vast consumption of timber.

Flora. Not at all—portable pillories, like long cravats, would distinguish the man of intrigue; and the harmless boy of the town would fee counsel to convict him, that he might not be out of fashion.

Fabio. 'Gad, I don't think they'd be unbecoming.

Flora. Then you don't intend to marry this poor devil?

Fabio. Faith I can't; they have nabb'd me at last.

Flora (with vexation). How! You are not married?

Fabio. Noosed, halter'd, egad a man might as well be pilloried.

Flora. Monster!—ha! ha! Pray, Sir, if I might presume—how came a man of your address to be so taken in?

Fabio. Why, Sir, hanging and marriage—If indeed they had only offer'd the halter I should have submitted; but when they came to propose the torture, 'gad I flinch'd, and was married.

Flora. Explain, Sir.

Fabio. Why, Sir; my master and I were taken in a late expedition by a body of Indians—poor I was condemn'd to the stake, that they might amuse themselves with my War Song—'Gad I had very little inclination to be jolly—whether they wou'd have put me in tune or no, I can't tell, for just as a delicate Squaw, about five feet eleven and a half, with a complexion fair as a Spanish olive, was advancing to make the first blow at me, struck with the beauty of my figure, she let fall her knotted club, and demanded my faithful hand in marriage.

Flora. So then you have given up all thoughts of this Flora?

Fabio. Yes; and my Indian spouse too.

D 2   SONG.

S O N G.   F A B I O.

Two maidens my heart transfix'd,
  One a lilly, one brown as a berry.
I stood like a boy betwixt
  A black and a white heart cherry.

One blush'd like the rose in the morning,
  Which in the garden blows;
And one like the rose adorning
  The shoes of our Garden-beaux.

My heart, now black, now white,
  Young Cupid laid his lash on;
I sobb'd, by day, and by night,
  With a kind of a pye-ball'd passion.

But now each beautiful lass
  Her forces marches away,
And I'm no longer an ass
  Between two bundles of hay.

Depriv'd of my white sweet-heart,
  And my black so seducing and mellow,
For the Garden again I'll depart,
  And pick up a juicy morella.

          [*Exeunt* Fabio *and* Flora.

S C E N E, *Fountain Garden.*

Enter Leonora, Julia, *and* Flora.

  Flora. Oh! Madam, I am in the right—I am
convinc'd.——
  Leonora. Have you seen my Garcias then?
                                        Flora.

Flora. No, Madam, but this is my villain, and a precious one he is! Oh Madam, Oh Lady Julia, I have difcovered fuch iniquity—I am fcarcely cool yet; yes, yes, Madam, only rely upon me, we are right, this muft be your Don Garcias, Madam, and no other.

Enter Don Juan, *and conceals himfelf behind a tree.*

Juan. Ah ha! have I caught you my Lady Julia falfe to me and with that young coxcomb! A pretty errand I am come on—to witnefs my own difgrace (*afide*).

Leonora. My fweet Julia, fhare my tranfports. (*Embracing her*).

Juan. Confufion!——

Julia. My charming friend.

Juan (afide.) Friend! Aye, that's the damn'd word with them all.

Julia. "In this moment of fufpence there is a foftnefs about you that is really bewitching."

Juan (afide.) "Bewitching!"

Julia. "And I think, if I could love another?— Heaven muft form for me, juft fuch a man, as you."

Juan (afide.) "If that is not pretty plump, the devil's in it."

Leonora. "Ha! ha! Upon my honour I believe you."

Juan (afide.) "The devil doubt you.—puppy.—"

Leonora. Now if Don Juan were here, down would he pop on his knees and devour your hand with kiffes.

Juan (afide). "He wou'd!"

Leonora. "And really I wifh he was here."

Juan. "You do." (*Afide*).

Leonora.

Leonora. " It is a pity fuch a delicate declaration of conflancy fhould be thrown away."

Juan. " Infolent coxcomb." (*Coming forward.*) " I can bear this foolery no longer"—but " I forget mylelf,"—if that perfidious girl difcovers me, I ruin my friend—I will fteal off and wait in another part of the garden till this puppy of a Lieutenant-Governor is alone. (*Afide.*) [*As he is going off* Fabio *meets him*].

Fabio. Ah! Signior Don Garcias! I fought you, Sir.

Juan. The devil take the fellow!—[Leonora, Julia, *and* Flora *turn round*].

Julia. Oh heavens! my Juan here!

Fabio (*to Flora.*) Signior Don Garcias of Guada-laxara, Sir.

Leonora. (*Afide.*) *This* Garcias?

Julia. Garcias?—ridiculous!

Flora. Pray, Sir, are you—is—is your name,—are you Don Garcias?

Juan. The fame, Sir.

Leonora. (*Afide.*) Then I am wretched!

Julia. Surely my eyes cannot deceive me fo much. Don Juan (*he affeits not to hear her*). You look, Sir, as if you never faw me before.

Juan. Moft probably I do, Madam, for I really do not recollect that I ever had that honour.

Julia. This is the moft extraordinary—I will not call it effrontery—then, Sir, I prefume I muft be mif-taken—you are not Don Juan de Zeneto?

Juan. That certainly, Madam, is not my name.

Julia. And you have not been formerly an officer in this garrifon.

Juan. If I have, Madam, I certainly did my duty in my fleep.

Julia. Then you did not three years ago fwear
the

the moſt ſolemn?—this is too much! (*burſts into tears*).

Juan. "I am exceedingly ſorry, Sir, for the miſtake which this Lady labours under."—May I preſume to aſk why I am admitted to the honour of attending your Lordſhip?

Leonora. This has been a day of miſtakes, Don Garcias: you have been miſtaken for a gentleman of the ſame name—who has fled from juſtice.

Julia (looking archly at him.) Then you never were here before, Sir.

Juan. Never, Madam.

Julia. I hope, Sir, you will meet with—much pleaſure in this ſtrange place.

Juan. Love—Madam—has—I ſee, taken poſſeſ-ſion of theſe groves, and his ſmiles muſt render them an Elyſium.

Leonora. You are a true Spaniard, I ſee—With-out love, indeed, nature has no beauties.

QUINTETTO.

Leo.   *The morning breeze which ſweeps the grove,*
      Its balmy perfume ſteals from love ;
      If ſweet the feather'd warbler's ſong,
      Its ſweeteſt notes to love belong.

DUETT.

Juan
&
Julia.
  { *But for the wretch condemn'd to feel*
  { *The mining doubt, the jealous fear,*
  { *No perfume o'er his ſenſes ſteal,*
  { *No muſic ſoothes his ſullen ear.*

FLORA.

FLORA.

What fate then shall the miscreant know,
Who perjur'd, profligate, and vain,
Derides an artless virgin's pain,
And basely triumphs in her woe ?

FABIO.

But bind him to the maid for life,
No breeze is wanting with a wife :
Eternal storms shall whistle round him,
And music's shrillest notes confound him.

CHORUS.

Love is compos'd of smiles and tears,
Of storms and calms, and hopes and fears.

END OF THE FIRST ACT.

ACT

A C T. II.

S C E N E I.

The outside of the Governor's Palace.

Don Juan *and* Fabio.

Juan. I AM determin'd to conceal myfelf fomewhere about the palace 'till I can find an opportunity
of feeing and upbraiding this inconftant girl, and
then——

Fabio. —Embark for Old Spain and leave her to
take root like a weeping willow on the fhore.

Juan. Do you think fhe wou'd weep?

Fabio. Like a rainy feafon, Sir,—depriv'd of the
genial rays of fuch a brilliant planet—Sir——

Juan. Oh! Mr. Fabio, your humble fervant.——
But may I not at laft have been deceiv'd—if fo—can
fhe ever forgive my behaviour?

Fabio. A lover's eye is not to be trufted, Sir.

Juan. Deceiv'd! Impoffible—did not I behold their
embraces?

Fabio. Perhaps they may be relations, Sir.

Juan. Relations!

Fabio. You know, Sir, her father is Governor,
and men in power always prefer their fons, or ne-
phews, or coufins, for the good of their country.

E,   SONG.

SONG. Fabio.

'Tis pleasant to see when my Lord obtains
A post in administration,
How the love of his country, which boils in his veins,
Infects each dear relation.
Up his cousins, flock by dozens,
One is proud of supporting a place,
Just that it may not fall into disgrace,
One wou'd finger the Treasury plumbs,
Just to keep him from biting his thumbs;
If they juggle for titles and such pretty things,
If they lie or they flatter for stars or for strings,
Oh! 'tis all for the good of the nation.

But shou'd my Lord at length for his pains
Be charg'd with peculation,
How his crime corrupts the pure blood in the veins
Of every dear relation.
Down his cousins, drop by dozens,
Then they find that a snug little place
May lie now and then in the road to disgrace,
That they had better been sucking their thumbs,
Than liming their fingers with Treasury plumbs,
And if some more resolv'd upon taking their swing,
Tho' their stars are eclips'd, find their end in a string,
Why, 'tis all for the good of the nation.

Juan. If I shou'd have been deceiv'd.—She will never pardon my conduct.

Fabio. Oh, Lord, Sir,—you won't remain at her feet two minutes and a half by a stop watch.—— She will scold first, pout next, and then be silent— then perhaps, before the flame of anger goes quite out, it will blaze—she will scold again—then—she will
                                                                                            let

let fall her hand by accident close to yours—you will
press it—she will struggle for it—you will kiss it—she
will be silent again—give you a side glance with a
gentle sigh—call herself an easy fool, and your pardon
is seal'd for ever.

Juan.   You seem to understand these things.

Fabio.   A susceptible heart, Sir,—'tis accidence,
grammar, and vocabulary on the subject.

Juan.   One of your brown Indian beauties, Mr.
Fabio?

Fabio.   Yes, Sir, I amused myself by engraving
my sweet lineaments on a piece of copper, and in return receiv'd such an impression!

Juan.   Of your own figure, Fabio?

Fabio.   You a lover and ask that, Sir?—'Tis the
way with us all—we amuse ourselves by painting our
own perfections on the heart of a mistress, and we
have no sooner taught the canvass to glow than we
fall in love with the picture—particularly if the frame
be handsome. This we call susceptibility in the lady,
and gratitude in ourselves.

Juan.   You are a satyrist, Sir.

Fabio.   This was admirably well illustrated, Sir,
by Terry Ma'gra, an Irish Serjeant in my master's
company and a great connoisseur in these matters—
by my soul, said he, I never could love any woman on
earth, 'till I had first found a return of my passion.

Enter Alkmonoak.

Alkm.   Don Juan, I sought you.—Your friend is
at home and very anxious to know the success of
your plan.—He seem'd to court solitude, and I left
him in hopes of meeting with you.

Juan.   Fabio, go to your master, tell him how
completely we have succeeded in regard to him——
however unlucky I have been myself!

Fabio.

Fabio. I fly, Sir.   [*Exit Fabio.*

Alkm. Then you have been unlucky, Don Juan?

Juan. Oh nothing extraordinary—a new inftance of the perfidy of the fex—that's all.—Come I am on duty here for fome time—ftroll with me and I will tell you all.—I find I muſt laugh at my misfortunes, Chief; for if I was to yield to them as Garcias and you do—what a charming fociety we ſhould compofe.

Alkm. The frowns of fortune I defpife as much as any man ; but in a breaſt like mine the wounds of love can never be clofed. The image of my Ifeagli is fo interwoven with my frame that nothing but death can tear it from my heart.

S O N G.

Thou that liv'ſt in every part,
In the bufy pulſe do'ſt beat ;
Panting in the faithful heart,
Glowing with the vital beat.

Can'ſt thou, mingled thus with life,
Ever ceaſe to warm the breaſt ;—
Never till this mortal ſtrife
Ending—gives the foul to reſt.

[Exeunt.

SCENE II.

Enter Secretary *and* Zempoalla.

Zemp. Then we are fafe from the Governor?

Secretary. Yes, yes, he is gone to fee your little Indian.

Zemp.

Zemp. Confufion feize him!

Secretary. You feem nettled this morning, mafter Chief.

Zemp. Have not I caufe? to have the moft delicious morfel revenge ever offer'd fnatch'd from me—the Chief Alkmonoak, a Chickafaw, my enemy, and that of the Spaniards—I exulted in the idea, of approaching vengeance—when the guard that I placed over him, in a fit of drunken phrenzy fir'd their huts; in the confufion he efcap'd me.

Secretary. Come, come, never mind the fweeteft morfel that revenge ever offer'd, what think you of the fweeteft morfel that love ever——

Zemp. My good Secretary! you can affift me further if you will——

Secretary. (*Touches the palm of his hand.*)

Zemp. Softly mafter Secretary, have not you receiv'd?——

Secretary. And have not I conniv'd? does not the town fwarm with your Indians whom I have admitted under the difguife of traders? Your pretence indeed is the carrying off this Indian wench Ifcagli—but there are enough of you to carry off the town — Shall I endanger my country for a few ounces of gold duft? Why I ufe it for fcouring fand.

Zemp. Had not you better apply it to your confcience.

Secretary. Humph!

Zemp. 'Tis Ifcagli I feek—your town is fafe, you may truft to my honour for that.

Secretary. Your honour!

Zemp. Yes, Commiffary, though a marketable commodity to the pale European.—To the fun-burnt Indian honour is a facred depofit.

Secretary. Come, come, Chief, what will you do now your men are in without my affiftance?——

Your

Your Indians are come under a pretence of trading;
they have brought furs with them.——

Zemp. True.——

Secretary. Rich?

Zemp. Of the finest quality.

Secretary. Good—I want to make a present to a
lady in Europe.

Zemp. You shall have your choice.

Secretary. I will conduct you to a spot which is a
favourite place of retirement of your Iscagli, from
which there is a private door leading into the very
pavilion which the fond Governor has built for her.——
I will use my authority to assist your escape through
the postern gate of the town—but I shall want a little
of your gold dust, just to scatter about and blind the
centries.

Zemp. You shall have it.

Secretary. Meet me in half an hour—farewel.——
You see Chief how much better it is to apply to the
fountain head, the Secretary—at once—without going
the round about way to him through his master.

(*Exeunt severally.*

SCENE III. *Iscagli's garden with a pavilion at a distance.*

Iscagli *with an* Indian Attendant.

Attend. Suppose lady, your love for the Chief
Alkmonoak, crown'd with success.

Iscagli. I thank thee for the thought, yet I shall
never see him more.

Attend. Would not you regret the comforts of
more polish'd society to which you have been of late
accustom'd?

Iscagli.

Iscagli. Is it thus you prophane the name of love?
have you forgot the leſſon I taught you the other
day?

Attend. No.

Iscagli. Repeat it then with me.

DUETT. ISCAGLI and ATTENDANT.

To ſhun the gay and gaudy bower,
 To ſeek the but obſcure and low,
To laugh at fame, to fly from power,
 If mighty love but will it ſo;
  Is but poorly to obey
  Paſſion's ſweet but rigid ſway.

To deem the flint a bed of down,
 The wild woods produce heavenly food,
To mock mankind's united frown,
 If ſuch to mighty love ſeem good,
  Is but poorly to obey
  Paſſion's ſweet but rigid ſway.

Iscagli. No, ye powers bear me witneſs! how
gladly would I forego the ſoftneſs of the ſplendid
couch for the fragrance of the ruſhy mat—the wretched imitating Theorbo for the ſweet ſong of the nightingale.—I would deck our humble wigwam for my
love's approach with all the variegated plumage of
our luxuriant Indian groves—It ſhou'd be my ozier
cage, and my love, my Alkmonoak, my ſweet bird
—he ſhould be my bird of paradiſe and convert my
hut into a Heaven.

I   *Enter*

Enter Don Lopez.

Don Lopez. Come to my arms, my little Angel, egad I was going to fay of light—but thy little brown fkin is but twilight at beft.

Ifcagli. Would it had not the misfortune to pleafe thee.

Don Lopez. Misfortune to pleafe me,—did you ever hear fuch a young devil—that gate open ftill, I fee you have been ftrolling about that confounded meadow.

Ifcagli. Why fhould your unreafonable jealoufy deny me the enjoyment of Nature's beauties?

Don Lopez. Nature's beauties!

Ifcagli. The diftant yellow cliff which fkirts the meadow hangs as if it liftened to the murmur of the ftream beneath it.

Don Lopez. Zounds! are there not gravel walks, and flower-pots, and fticks, with lobfters claws upon them; and for exotics is there not a pot of Dutch dandelion which with the affiftance of only two gardeners looks almoft as well as when it firft came over.

Ifcagli (with a difgufted air). This garden is regularity itfelf.

Don Lopez. And I mean to keep you within the bounds of regularity.

Ifcagli. What right have you to confine me?

Don Lopez. No great right, but I love you fo!—

Ifcagli. Forbear to teaze me thus in vain.

Don Lopez. Befides, there is the Chief Zempoalla in town, "who knows but he or fome of his myrmidons may fnap you up in one of your favourite walks."

Ifcagli. "The hated Zempoalla in town!"

Don Lopez. Ay, and if the dog fhould carry you off!

Ifcagli.

Iscagli. "It is impossible without your knowledge."

Don Lopez. " I don't know that—he was with me this morning and terribly savage about you I can tell you." Egad it would break my heart; for your poor little Governor does so love you. *(Takes hold of her hand).*

Iscagli. Do not torment me.

Don Lopez. Zounds, how can I help it—I don't run headlong into love, but love flows in upon me— Come, my little Cocoa-Nut, do be kind.—Only conceive, a Governor, and a Governor like me too. —Egad you should live like a princess—in my own palace—You should be any thing but my wife—but for an old Christian—'gad, conceive that—to marry a young fucking Christian—a Christian of four years old at most—'gad it won't do.

Iscagli. I am glad of it—for I cannot love you.

Don Lopez. Egad, now I think of it, you shall remain within these walls—till that fellow is fairly out of town.

Iscagli. To confine me is not the way to increase my attachment towards you.

Don Lopez. Zounds, you will not love me if I give you your liberty.

Iscagli. I shall love you better than if you confine me.

Don Lopez. My sweet little Indian Nightingale! I can deny you nothing—but harkee, keep a good look out, post your female centries—send out your petticoat vedettes, watch like a lynx.

Iscagli. Fear not—I should be more wretched with Zempoalla—than—than——

Don Lopez. With me!—Much oblig'd to you.

F   *Enter*

Enter Servant.

Servant. I beg pardon, my Lord, for breaking in upon your privacy.

Don Lopez. Well, Sir.

Servant. Your Lordship's Secretary waits—he wishes to communicate something of importance which concerns the Lady Julia. [*Exit.*

Don Lopez. Zounds! who wou'd be plagu'd with a daughter, sure the devil is in me for a Governor! I sit down every day to a sumptuous table, and am sure to lose my appetite before I come to the thing I like best—I place my affections on a tawny wench whom other men wou'd despise, and she chuses to hate me—I have a particular inclination to govern an unruly daughter, and I am Governor over every thing in the whole city but her.—Farewell, my little Nightingale, keep a good look out. [*Exit.*

Ixcagli. Now for my favourite spot of contemplation, not perhaps less favoured because forbidden.

S O N G.

There to muse and there to sigh,
There to sit and think on love ;
There with contemplation's eye
Over happier scenes to rove :
There to bid the shadowy train
Of former transports live again.

[*Exeunt.*

S C E N E IV. *Leonora's Garden.*

Leonora *and* Julia.

Julia. If I shou'd meet my Juan—if I shou'd find him still faithful—yet I have my father's insatiate ava-

1   rice

rice to combat——would I were the pooreſt peaſant of my native Arragonian Hills rather than the ſplendid victim I now am.

SONG. Juɪɪᴀ.

When the blythe village maid leads her flock to the plains,
  Ah me! how I envy her lot:
I'd ſpurn all the ſplendor a palace contains,
  With freedom to dwell in a cot.
Awak'd by the lark, o'er my Love as I hung,
  His ſlumbers I'd chaſe with a kiſs;
No tyrant to check me, no venomous tongue
  With ſlander to ſully my bliſs.

The toil of the day wou'd be pleaſure to me,
  Still drinking freſh health from the gale,
And evening wou'd bring, with an aſpect of glee,
  The legend, the ſong, or the tale:
Till the ſtill gloom of night wrapt the hamlet in reſt,
  And my fancy grew big with alarms,
Then I'd ſteal to my Lover, creep cloſe to his breaſt,
  And loſe all my fears in his arms.

Leonora. Come come, Julia, find but your Juan, and we will bring about the reſt——" it is hard if two of us are not a match for your old father."

Julia. I ſhall find him in Don Garcias of Guadalaxara: " I ſaw him but this moment from the corner of your terrace which looks towards my father's palace—he was walking under the garden wall which fronts my apartment with an Indian Chief, and as a perſon advanc'd towards the ſpot where they ſtood, they both retir'd into the little grove on the right of the wall."

F 2

Leonora.

Leonora. Well, be but patient, my dear—your doubts will all be diffipated.——'Tis now fome time fince I difpatch'd a ferjeant with a file of men to bring this Gentleman before us—but recollect that I confented to this ftretch of power.——

Julia. To fatisfy my impatience. I know it, my fweet friend :—but—my dear—I have a ftrange inclination juft to walk to the terrace.

Leonora. Poor Julia !

Julia. To tell you the truth I am rather anxious about a letter.

Leonora. A letter !—what you could not wait till he was brought here—according to your own defire too, Julia.

Julia. What fhall I fay—I am a foolifh girl—but I thought he might flip through your hands. I wifh to watch him a little left my page fhould have mifs'd him——Will you walk towards the terrace ?

Leonora. Excufe me, my dear,—I can wait till he is brought here.

Julia. Ah ! Leonora you are no lover.

Leonora. " No Lover *(fighs)*—why will you force me to recollect what I am ?—The dawn of this day, Julia, fmiled upon my almoft forgotten hopes—Heaven grant that its clofe may at leaft fee my friend happy."

Julia. " I thank you fincerely,"—then you will not walk ?

Leonora. I will wait for you here—if this Gentleman, whether Don Juan or Don Garcias, is not yet in cuftody, we have time enough. [*Exit* Julia.] No lover ! Ah Julia ! how little do you know with what painful emotions the remembrance of that fad night which faw me torn for ever from my fondeft hopes even now fills my bofom.

Enter

Enter Don Garcias *attended by a serjeant.*

Garcias. I underſtand, Sir, that you are the Lieutenant-Governor.

Leonora. Oh heavens! what do I ſee! has my
imagination rais'd this phantom? For heaven's ſake,
whence come you?

Garcias. Sir!

Leonora. Why did you not come when I firſt
ſent for you? You little know the diſquiet you have
cauſed me.

Garcias. Surely, Sir, there muſt be ſome miſtake—I——

Leonora. I have indeed been miſtaken—your name
is——

Garcias. Garcias——why I am here my attendant
can inform you better than I.

Leonora (*to the ſoldier.*) Walk apart.—Don Garcias I expected to have ſeen you when I firſt ſent.

Garcias. My Lord, I am aſham'd of the decep-
tion—the danger of my ſituation induc'd a valued
friend to aſſume my name before you; when your
late order came to arreſt me that friend was abſent;
I ſaw the impropriety of ſubjecting him to farther
inconvenience, and ſurrender'd myſelf.

Leonora. That friend was Don Juan de Feneto?

Garcias. I find, my Lord, that our plot has been
detected.

Leonora. I am ſorry for you, Don Garcias.——
Your appearance is not unprepoſſeſſing—I was betray'd into—ſome ſurprize at your firſt entrance from
——from—the difficulty—I felt in believing you to be
the man againſt whom ſo foul a charge has been
preferr'd.

Garcias. That I am the man, is as true as the
charge

charge itfelf is falfe. I am more unfortunate than guilty, my only crime has been excefs of love.

Leonora.   You have lov'd—then ?

Garcias.   Almoft to madnefs.

Leonora.   " The object of this fatal paffion—

Garcias.   " I once thought an angel.

Leonora.   " She prov'd—

Garcias.   " A very woman !

Leonora.   " Nay then—I pity you."

Garcias.   I once beheld with little lefs than ado-ration, the purity of that foul, which has been fince contaminated with the fouleft crimes—but hence un-manly weaknefs ! here I folemnly vow never to think of her difhonour'd form again, but with—(*going to kneel*)—

Leonora (*catches his arm.*) Love ! Garcias. (Don Garcias *ftarts and furveys with furprize*) Ha ! ha ! ha ! no rafh vows, Don Garcias—no rafh vows !—but indeed it is immaterial what you think of the poor girl now.——You facrific'd her I perceive to your jealoufy.

Garcias.   By my honour I never facrific'd her.—" For aught I know, fhe lives and paffes this very hour in infamy."

Leonora.   " Perhaps in honour, Garcias, and per-haps in blifs—Pardon me, Don Garcias, the Lady may be very happy you know notwithftanding her offence, ha ! ha !"

Garcias.   Give me leave to tell you, *Sir*, this mirth——

Enter Julia, *rufhing in, ftarts back, and curtfies gravely to* Leonora.

Julia.   Oh my—my Lord !——Your Lordfhip is engag'd.

                                        Leonora.

Leonora. This, Madam, is Don Garcias of——
Garcias. Valentia, Madam.

Leonora. Moſt true!—but Julia—*(taking her aſide)* —you look alarm'd, my dear.

Julia. I am ruin'd, I ſaw my father from the terrace coming this way with a letter in his hand, and by his rage I am ſure it is the letter I wrote to Juan.

Leonora. Don Garcias, do you know of Don Juan's receiving a letter this morning?

Garcias. That letter was deliver'd to me by miſtake, and is now in poſſeſſion of a perſon who met the party, which eſcorted me hither, and whom I underſtood to be the Governor's Secretary.

Enter Flora and Fabio.

Flora. My Lord—the Governor is coming this way.

Leonora. Whom have you there, Sebaſtian?

Garcias. 'Tis my ſervant, my Lord.

Fabio. Your Lordſhip ſees I follow the fortunes of my maſter.

Flora. From Guadalaxara even to New Spain.

Enter Don Lopez.

Don Lopez. Who the devil wou'd be curs'd with a daughter!

Leonora. What is the matter, Sir?

Don Lopez. There—read—no—now I think on't ——I'll read myſelf—

(Reads) "If Don Juan will walk on the ramparts—"
Zounds, he ſhall cool his heels there,
 " at ſeven o'clock he will meet"——
With a corporal and a file of men, I promiſe him:
then

then bye and bye there's a long ftroke and a dot, and then a dafh and then fo prettily.———

" But muft not fhe collect from what has paffed that he does not defire to fee his Julia."

How mincingly the jade lyes, fhe knows fhe lyes; and the letters are all curl'd up into a fneer—they have an ironical twift in them—Come, come, Madam, I'll take care that you don't attend this affignation: I'll fecure you at leaft.

Leonora. Come, let me talk to her, my Lord; you know I am to be trufted with her.

Don Lopez. Yes, and I believe you are the only young fellow in Mexico that is——If you talk to her, you muft talk to her in her own apartments though; for I'll take care fhe fha'n't get out of them——Who is that?

Leonora. Don Garcias, Sir.

Don Lopez. A terrible looking dog—He has murder in his very countenance.

Leonora. I honour your difcernment, Sir.

QUINTETTO.

LEONORA.

How keen that glance which in the face
The vices of the heart can trace;
Yet fure thofe eyes lefs ftrongly prove
The fway of lawlefs rage than love.

CHORUS.

And he can fcarcely guilty prove
Who's only crime's excefs of love.

Don

Don Lopez.

Zounds, leave me alone to discover a knave,
I'm fully aware there's some nicety in it;
But let them play off all the tricks that they have,
I'm down on the rascals in less than a minute.

Garcias.

What ever crimes upon my face
   Your keen discernment loves to trace,
Too sure my fatal tale will prove
   My only crime excess of love.
And be can, &c.

Fabio.

To solve your enigma permission I crave,
If right I divine, this is all that is in it,
If his lordship is anxious to find out a knave,
We have but to leave him alone for a minute.

Julia.

My father, look upon this face,
   Whose smiles thou once wert fond to trace,
And there let thy discernment prove
   My only crime excess of love.

And she can scarcely guilty prove
Whose only crime's excess of love.

[Exeunt Don Lopez and Leonora leading Julia
Flora, Serjeant, &c. with Garcias and Fabio
in custody].

END OF THE SECOND ACT.

G   A C T

ACT III.

SCENE I.

A beautiful meadow, on one fide a garden wall with a pavilion—a door from the pavilion open. Ifcagli difcover'd feated on a projecting part of, and leaning againft, a cliff, on which fhe is tracing with the point of an arrow the name of Alkmonoak.

(An Indian Attendant waiting).

SONG. Iscagli.

THOU fandy bourne, upon whofe faithlefs breaft
I leave my lover's facred name imprefs'd;
Sweep but the breeze! or fall the fainting fhower,
We find thee printlefs in a little hour.
But tears and fighs in vain for years effay,
To bear his Image from my heart away.

What is the Governor's idle intelligence worth? No Indians appear.

Attend. If this Indian, Zempoalla, is lurking in town you cannot furely be too cautious.

Ifcagli. If he were to fucceed, I fhould indeed exchange my prefent flavery for a worfe—are fome of our people on the watch?

Attend. I have fo placed them, that no one can approach us without our receiving early intelligence.

Ifcagli.

Ifcagli. Sing me the fong of the fair European who died for love.——

Attend. The fong I learn'd of the Englifh foldier?

Ifcagli. Yes.

SONG. (By Attendant.)

What boots it where thy foldier lies?
Fond regret is folly;
O'er the files why ftray your eyes?
Weeping, widow'd Polly.

On the bridge thy Henry fell,
I may fall to-morrow,
His death became a foldier well,
Mourner check thy forrow.

E'er night her forrows funk to reft,
Pale grew the rofe of beauty;
And cold the hand her foldier preft,
When call'd, at dawn, on duty.

Enter an Attendant.

2d Attend. Lady provide for your fafety—as we ftood on the watch we difcover'd an Indian Chief, who, the moment he faw us, advanc'd haftily.

Attend. Indeed you had better go in.

Ifcagli. We fhall retire to the gate neareft the palace, that if any danger fhould occur we may inform the Governor.   (*They enter the door of the pavilion, and fhut it after them.*)

Enter Alkmonoak.

Alkm. This feems the land of enchantment—the wild charms of the fpot which feduc'd me from the

fide of my friend wou'd fanction the idea.—Thefe
females too, who like me, feem natives of this foil, at
my approach flit from my fight. (*Looking at the feat
which Ifcagli has quitted*).   This feems the feat of contemplation itfelf.——Sacred heavens! what do I fee?
the name of the wretched Alkmonoak, (*taking up the
arrow which Ifcagli left leaning againft the cliff*), this arrow too is of the form us'd in our nation.—Such have I
poffefs'd, plumed by the hand of Ifcagli herfelf, from
the wing of the nightingale.—Surely my Ifcagli was
among the women who fled at my approach—for
what but the hand of love has traced in this unknown
fpot the name of the haplefs Alkmonoak.—If it was
indeed my Ifcagli fhe is within thefe walls: will they
deny admiffion to a fond and faithful lover?

Enter Zempoalla, *with Indians of his party.*

Zemp.   This is the pavilion which the fond Governor has built for her—here let us conceal ourfelves
till the fhades of evening approach—but foft, fome
perfon comes this way—by all my hopes of vengeance 'tis my enemy Alkmonoak, perdition feize
him, at this moment perhaps he quits the arms of
the wanton Ifcagli.

Alkmonoak *advances.*

Alkm.   If fhe is in this pavilion my voice may
reach her ear.

S O N G.   ALKMONOAK.

*Do thou fweet fympathy my voice convey
Through thofe deaf walls a lover's ear to win,*

So

So hovering round this tenement of clay
Some kindred spirit wakes the soul within.

(Zempoalla *makes signs to the Indians who seize*
Alkmonoak.)

CHORUS of Indians.

Away! away! thee tortures wait
Nor can'st thou shun thy destin'd fate.

ALKMONOAK.

Thus, at the dawn of hope's mild day,
    The flattering prospect to forego,
To see the shadow flit away,
    Chang'd for the greisly front of woe!

ZEMPOALLA.

Thou bated Chief! thee tortures wait.

ALKMONOAK.

Then welcome every shaft of fate.

CHORUS.

Away! away! thee tortures wait,
Nor can'st thou shun thy destin'd fate.

SCENE II.

Flora (Fabio *with his arms pinion'd*) *and soldiers.*

Flora. I have order'd these men to attend you to
the town-hall where the Governor will proceed on

2   the

the trial of your master and you; from what I can
hear of your case—there is little hope—your time is
come.

Fabio. 'Tis not *welcome*, I am sure! I wish to
my soul it wou'd *go* again.

Flora. Console yourself as well as you can, friend,
about this time to-morrow, in all human probability,
you will be at peace.

Fabio. Egad, I had rather be at war as little as I
like it.—But what a cursed country is this, where an
innocent man—oh! it goes to my heart—I wish I had
been guilty to deserve death—I have a strange disin-
terestedness about me—I would not have more than
I merit—to-morrow did you say?

Flora. Certainly to-morrow.

Fabio. Sure some time should be allowed a man
for preparation.

Flora. Oh! you must be prepar'd; Religion and
you are old acquaintance.

Fabio. Very old indeed, but the connection has
been drop'd ever since I was thirteen years of age,—
'twill require some time to renew our acquaintance.

Flora. Till to-morrow morning, will not that be
time enough?

Fabio. Not by years, I am such a shy rogue,
(*Pauses and utters a long groan*). Oh,—Oh!——

Flora. You seem in high spirits, cou'd not you
give us a song?

Fabio. A song! do you take me for a swan to
sing when I'm dying? Egad I'm more like a turkey
truss'd for the spit.—But, Sir, I can't raise my (*makes
a motion as if he wish'd to raise his arms*) voice while I
am pinion'd so—I'm a game cock, Sir, I can't crow
without flapping my wings.

Flora. Come, it may be in my power to serve
you; sing me a good laughing song, now.

Fabio.

Fabio. A what?

Flora. A laughing fong.

Fabio. A laughing fong! 'gad if I do laugh it will be on the wrong fide of my mouth.

Flora. Sing: if you value my friendfhip.

Fabio. (*Sings in a melancholy tone*):

" *Now's the time for mirth and glee, &c.*"

Flora. Very well done.

Fabio. D'ye think fo, Sir? I wifh you'd releafe me then; for mine are " Native wood notes wild," and I fhall never be able to fing in a cage.

Flora. Serjeant, attend this Gentleman to the town-hall, I fhall examine you myfelf firft, and if you conceal nothing——

Fabio. Nothing, upon my honour.

Flora. I may obtain for you——

Fabio. A reprieve?——

Flora. A choice as to the manner of your funeral.

[*Exeunt.*

* S C E N E III. Julia's *Chamber, in the* Governor's *Palace.*

Julia *in* Leonora's *cloaths, and* Leonora *in* Julia's.

Julia. I fcarcely know myfelf—do I walk boldly; is my ftrut pretty martial?—it won't look particular juft to keep my hand on the hilt of my fword —fo—or it will certainly throw me down.

* It became neceffary, from fome circumftances attending the firft reprefentation, that this fcene fhould undergo fome alteration. It is here printed as it originally ftood.

Leonora.

Leonora. Then you will fall by the sword as a soldier ought.

Julia. I declare you are in such spirits I hardly know you——but, my dear Leonora, for Heaven's sake do not stalk so—remember you have forsworn the man for ever.

Leonora. For ever—It is become a very useless character since I have found my Garcias——but, my dear, you seem to have forgotten the cause of our changing dresses.

Julia. That I might escape from my father, and fly to my Juan.

Leonora. The sooner you put your design in execution the better, I should think.

Julia. True, but what will you do?

Leonora. Leave me to coax your old father—— a pretty woman never fail'd with him yet.

Julia. Now I come to the point, I am a coward.

Leonora. A coward! I positively will not have my cloaths disgrac'd;—go directly to my house.—— Flora will introduce you to Don Garcias; make him acquainted with our story, and you will not be long in finding out Don Juan. *(Looking out)* As I live this seems the most lucky moment fate could offer you; the servants who were plac'd to guard you have left the saloon, and are running to and fro, in the utmost confusion.——Some person comes this way: a stranger too——

Julia. O Lud! O Lud! Let us conceal ourselves *(going into the closet)*.

Leonora. What again—for shame!

Julia. You are a perfect lion—would you had your skin again. *(Runs into a closet)*.

(Leonora retires to the back of the stage, and lets down her veil).

Enter

Enter Don Juan.

Juan. After prowling fo long round this curfed palace, I have at laft gain'd admittance, in the midft of a diabolical confufion, the caufe of which I cannot guefs.—This fuite of rooms fhould lead to the left wing, which my Julia inhabits—*my* Julia!—no, hold good Don Juan, fhe is none of your's—that curfed meffage to the Lieutenant-Governor!—What the women fee in thefe pale-fac'd puppies I cannot think —I look'd at him, and to my mind—he is a contemptible ill-looking young rafcal—an ugly dog.

(As he is fpeaking Leonora *fteals from behind and taps him on the fhoulder)*

My Julia!—No, you are not mine—I fuppofe, Madam, you overheard what I faid of the coxcomb who has fupplanted me.—After fo long an abfence to find! —Ungrateful girl——but I may have been deceiv'd; —do, my dear girl, tell me, for pity's fake, tell me why I found you with the Lieutenant-Governor this morning?——Will you not anfwer me? *(Leonora turns from him.)* Come, I do begin to think you are innocent——I have been fufpicious—jealous if you will, without caufe.

Leonora (turning from him, in a low voice.) Signior, Don Garcias.

Juan. How!

Leonora. What is the reafon, Sir, of your intrufion here?

Juan. Don Garcias!

Leonora. And what do you mean by talking in riddles thus?

Juan. Riddles! why, you will not have the barbarity to perfuade me that you do not know your Juan?

Leonora. You, Don Juan! there is fome like-
H   nefs

nefs indeed—now I think on it, I took you for Don
Juan, this morning—but you foon perfuaded me to
the contrary.

Juan.   There fhe has me—then you really affect
not to know me ?

Leonora.   Pardon me, Sir——I know you very
well; I faw you at the Lieutenant-Governor's this
morning.

Juan.   And never before ?

Leonora.   Never, upon my honour.

Juan.   Never?

Leonora.   Never.

Juan.   Will you drive me mad, Julia ! then you
have not even fo long as four years ago deign'd to
liften—to the declaration of that paffion which your
charms—had——

Leonora.   Four years ago'!—O Lud ! if ever I faw
you till this morning, may I be branded as the moft
faithlefs of my fex.

Juan.   I take you at your word——

    (Julia *opens the clofet door and he bears her*)
Damnation ! what do I fee—Conceal'd in her chamber !—falfe, falfe woman !——Come forth, Sir, or I
will tear you from your lurking-place—nor rank, nor
power fhall protect you—Draw, Sir !

Leonora.   Hold, Sir, a word: (*unveils*) be *ftarts
back and looks on* Julia, *who takes off her bat, and makes
him a low bow*).

Juan.   Am I in my fenfes ?

Julia.   After your kind fufpicions, Sir, I fuppofe
you will not believe that I made thefe preparations
to elope with you (*to* Juan).

Juan.   Pardon ! Pardon Julia !—but the Lieutenant-Governor——

Leonora.   The ugly dog is here, Sir.

Enter

Enter Flora.

Flora. Where is the Lieutenant-Governor?

Juan. *(pointing to* Leonora, *and surveying* Flora *attentively)* Here——Sir!

Flora. Arm! Arm, Sir, directly; I come with orders from the Governor to beat to arms.

Leonora. I believe, Don Juan, I must appoint you my deputy.

Juan. You will do me honour.

Leonora. My Aid de Camp shall attend you; Sebastian we give the command of the troops to Don Juan *(to Julia)* unless, Sir, you chuse.

Julia. Oh Heavens! not I.

Juan. Let me first conduct you to a place of safety.

Leonora. We can be no where more safe than here?—Where is the Governor?

Flora. At the Town Hall. He went there for the purpose of examining Don Garcias.

Leonora. There, Don Juan, when the tumult has subsided, we may meet.

Juan. Adieu, Madam—till then, my Julia, farewell.

[*Exeunt* Don Juan *and* Flora, Leonora *and* Julia.

SCENE IV.

Enter Don Lopez, Iscagli, *and* Secretary.

Don Lopez. As I'm a Governor, I thought they had got my little wild squirrel here—when I heard that terrible dog Zempoalla had taken a prisoner, I thought he had laid his claws upon thee; but the villain shou'd have fought through the whole garri-

son

son for thee, I promise him. I will not trust thee out of my sight again—Come, we will go into the balcony and see this Indian prisoner.

Iscagli. Not for worlds! I know too well the savage manners of our people—their barbarous tri-umphs, even whilst I liv'd amongst them, often shook my frame with agony——

Don Lopez. Pooh! Pooh!—they will only tickle him a little here; they will reserve his execution for a bonne-bouche when they get home.

Secretary. Had not the Lady better partake of the bonne-bouche too?

Don Lopez. 'Gad I like your feelings, Mr. Com-missary; poison and starvation, but no blood—Ma-nage your wife when you get her, and leave me to myself.

Secretary. To be plain with you, Sir, I think that will not be in a hurry.

Don Lopez. How Sir!

Secretary. Why, Sir, I begin to think that this Don Juan is a handsome young fellow of quality.— Now, Sir, though your daughter and I may become of the same flesh, the Pope himself can never make us of the same blood.—I shall be Donna'd out of the play.

Don Lopez. Well.

Secretary. " Were you at Donna Julia's last night —Donna Julia is of our party—Oh Sir, I'm sure Donna Julia will subscribe—We had a little supper at Donna Julia's on Sunday"—then comes this pithy question—" Did you ever see the wretch her hus-band ?"

Don Lopez. Very right.

Secretary. I shall be her meer night-cap, worn for convenience and thrown by on the appearance of company; or if by chance detected, ridiculed, com-
mented

mented on, *cut-up*, and at laſt voted incorrigible, and a new one recommended.

Don Lopez. " Pray, Sir, with proper ſubmiſſion to your high rank and exalted ſituation, may I aſk how long you have maintained this opinion ?

Secretary. " Ever ſince I have ſeen Don Juan."

Don Lopez (*lifting up his cane.*) Get out of my preſence, you mongrel, you muſhroom, you dung-hill nettle, get out, or by St. Anthony !——

Secretary. Zounds, Sir, is this treatment for a man with an hundred thouſand piſtoles in his pocket ?

Don Lopez. Raſcal! it vexes me to the ſoul that I have ever liſtened to propoſals which reflect ſo much diſgrace upon me—Come, my little Olive—do go to the balcony juſt to ſee the fight.

Iſcagh. Why will you preſs me to what is ſo un-pleaſing ? I delight not in ſcenes of miſery.

Don Lopez. Sure I am a Governor born to be diſobey'd. I infiſt upon your coming with me ; odds heart, I am almoſt afraid to truſt you out of my fight.

[*Exeunt.*

SCENE V.

Opens and diſcovers an open place before the town-hall ſur-rounded with palms, plantations, &c. In the front of the hall is a grand ſtair-caſe, with a gallery.

Zempoalla, Indians, and Alkmonoak chain'd.

SONG. ALKMONOAK.

The ſun ſets in night, and the ſtars ſhun the day,
But glory remains when their lights fade away ;
Begin, ye tormentors, your threats are in vain,
For the ſon of Alkmonoak ſhall never complain.

Remember

Remember the wood where in ambush we lay,
And the scalps which we bore from your nation away;
When the flame rises fast--you'll exult in my pain,
But the son of Alkmonoak shall never complain.

I go to the land where my father is gone,
His ghost shall rejoice in the fame of his son:
Death comes like a friend, he relieves me from pain,
And thy son, O Alkmonoak, has scorn'd to complain.

CHORUS of INDIANS.

" Where the forest deep and dread
" Mocks the sun with endless shade,
" Save amid the matted twine,
" Where the dog-snake basks supine;
" Through the gloom unhallow'd where,
" We mark the sullen eye-ball glare;
" As the tiger thwarts our way,
" Crouching low in cruel play;
" Where the she-bear licks her brood;
" Where the yell, which shakes the wood,
" Betrays the wolf, with famine gaunt,
" Lies the hunters dangerous haunt.

1st INDIAN.

In his ambush, wisely dark,
Scarce distinguish'd from the bark,
As he peeps beside a tree,
Our ruddy painted foe we see,
Hark, he took a deadly aim,
My comrade falls, revenge is fame.
Now the tomahawk I throw,
In vain the Chieftain flies the blow,

From

From him, panting as be lies,
The scalp I bear, the victor's prize.
This is war, advance, advance,
Join the warrior's glorious dance.

CHORUS.

This is war,—advance, advance,
Join the warrior's glorious dance.

(*A War Dance*):

Don Lopez *and* Ifcagli *appear on the stair-cafe, be dragging ber forward, she turns ber face form the stage.*

Don Lopez. Here they are! here they are! do but look, Ifcagli—was ever fuch a perverfe jade—oh! that I fhould love a wench with fuch a tafte.—In Europe now they will go fifty miles to fee a man hang'd, and this is worth a hundred of it. Odds heart —twift that abominable—pretty neck this way—I infift upon it.

Ifcagli. (*She turns round, and fees* Alkmonoak, *ftarts*). Sacred powers, my Alkmonoak, Alkmonoak!

Alkm. Who names Alkmonoak? (*feeing ber*) Ha! Ifcagli!

Ifcagli. Ye pitying powers! do I exift—my Lord! my life! my love! (*Rufhes down the ftair-cafe into* Alkmonoak's *arms.*)

Zemp. Confufion! what do I fee?

Ifcagli. Chief! you know me of your tribe.

Zemp. I do, and claim you.

Ifcagli. Hold!—the prifoner of war is at the difpofal of the woman who fhall chufe to refcue him by uniting herfelf to him in marriage—I defire to unite

I   my

my fate with that of your prisoner, and claim him as my husband.

Don Lopez. Hold! hold! this must not be?

Zemp. It shall not, Indians, guard well your prisoner; as to this woman, thus I claim her.

[*Seizing Iscagli.*

Don Lopez. Eh? Hold, zounds! that must not be neither—hark ye, Chief?

Zemp. Proceed I say.

Alkm. Villians forbear—— [*As they are going off.*

Enter Don Juan, Flora, *and* Spanish soldiers; *behind them* Leonora *and* Julia.

Juan. Surround those Indians and secure them.

Zemp. " Where is the other party which I sent to meet us at the gate?"

Juan. " Prisoners as you are,"—unbind the captive there, my friend Alkmonoak.

Alkm. How can I thank thee? twice hast thou given me life—once more than life! See, my friend, my lov'd, my lost Iscagli.

Juan. Your arms will be restor'd to you when you quit the town (*to Zempoalla*).

Don Lopez. Your most obedient humble servant, Sir. And pray who the devil are you?—ha! Don Juan, I kiss your hand; pray, Sir, who commissioned you? Who gave you command here?

Flora. I, Sir.

Don Lopez. You, Sir! and pray where is?——

Flora. The culprits, Sir, whom you ordered down to trial are now approaching.

Enter Garcias *and* Fabio *in custody.*

Garcias. " Which is the Governor?

Don

Don Lopez. "I am, Sir, at your service.—Egad these people don't know a Governor in the open air, where every fellow wears his hat.—You are Don Garcias?

Garcias. I am.

Don Lopez. Don Garcias you have murder'd the beauteous Leonora.

Garcies. I lov'd—but never wrong'd her.

Don Lopez. "Well, well, that you'll answer hereafter,"—you must go prisoner to Spain.

Juan. Here is a witness, my Lord, who will probably save him the trouble of so long a journey.

Don Lopez. What, hang him directly! 'gad I don't know whether it won't be the best way.

Flora. May it not by chance exceed your Lordship's authority?

Don Lopez. Where is your Commander, Mr. Aid-de-Camp? I'll have your authority superseded in a trice. Don Ferdinand—'gad I did not see you—do you hear all this.

Julia. (*Bows with confusion*).

Don Lopez. What the devil's the matter with you, 'gad now I think of it—how did you leave my daughter?

Julia. Trembling, lest she shou'd prove deceiv'd in the hope she has cherish'd of a father's indulgence. (Don Juan *takes her hand and they kneel to* Don Lopez).

Don Lopez. Wonder upon wonder!—take her Don Juan, I see there's no keeping her from you,— "besides I have chang'd my mind since I last saw that rascally Secretary."

Garcias. Juan, you would not mock me in this situation—can you assist me?

Juan. Will your Lordship indulge me by examining this witness?

I   *Don*

Don Lopez. With all my heart——what have you to fay, Madam ?

Leonora (lifts her veil.) " Don Garcias, do you know this face ?"

Garcias. Know it !

Leonora. " Does it betray an heart contaminated with the foulest crimes ?"

Garcias. " It fhould not—Oh Leonora !"

Leonora. Garcias, on that fatal night when we agreed to fly from Valentia, why did you not meet us, oppofite to the South Baftion ?

Garcias. The arguments of my Moorifh flave, Sadi, induc'd me to prefer the Weftern, and I fent you notice of it by him.

Leonora. Which we never receiv'd.

Garcias. Ha ! I perceive his treachery.

Leonora. " Seduc'd by the arts of this unprincipled confidant into his power, the hand of Providence alone refcued me from horrors at the bare remembrance of which I ftill fhudder."

Garcias. Oh Leonora; " my heart beats in tumult ; thought crowds on thought, and love, predominating love alone, refcues me from diftraction," —Can you forgive the credulous fool who has been the caufe ?——

Leonora. Of this moment's infupportable blifs (*rufhing into his arms*).

Don Lopez. A plaguy forward witnefs this !—— " 'Gad this is very pretty, but I don't fee what it has to do with the caufe."—Where is this whimfical Lieutenant-Governor ?—in his cuftody came the prifoner—and I fhall remand him—

Leonora. To the fame cuftody again from which, if he ever efcapes !—Do not you know me, Sir ?

Don Lopez. What a plague.—Yes, I think I do.
            —Why

—Why, damn it, has mine been a petticoat government after all? *(They confer aside)*.

Fabio. 'Gad, Mr. Aid-de-Camp, I have been looking at you this hour, and I begin to smell a rat.

Flora. If you suspect but half the truth, my friend, you had better make your escape—"Odds my life I have a great mind to take advantage of my cloth, and rid the world of such an heart-breaker—*(to Don Garcias)* do, Sir, lend the miscreant your sword. *(To Julia)* Sir, will you be my second?

Fabio. "Perish the weapons of war—you have my punishment in your hands—"—Marry me.

Flora. Soft, Mr. Fabio, what's to become of your Indian spouse?

Fabio. Zounds! my Squaw. I had forgot her—but we have parted for ever—so you and I, now,—eh?

Flora. I! I resolve never to see you more.

Fabio. You do—Zounds then I'm black-ball'd on both sides.

(Don Lopez and Leonora come forward.)

Don Lopez. Well, well, this is surprising, that I, "a wise Governor," shou'd not find you out,—Odds my life—I must revenge myself by a hearty buss.—*(Kisses Leonora)*.

Garcias. "Don Juan, joy to you—my brave Chief, accept my congratulations."

Don Lopez. Hold! hold! not so fast; I am not to lose my little wild Filbert so.

Leonora. My dear! dear Governor, you are too gallant a man to part two Lovers.—Come, let me plague you for once into a good action.—"I shall scarcely lose my favour with the Viceroy by the change in my sex—I must write to him on the occasion. I wish to speak well of you"—Enable me to

say

say that there is at least one Governor who has sacri-
fic'd his passions at the altar of justice.

Don Lopez.　Well, then,

Zemp.　" This, Lord Governor, is a breach of
the treaty between us.

Don Lopez.　" 'Tis but forcing you to do that
which your laws command—Come, come, Chief,
you are an honest man, and will soon feel as I do, that
when the performance of a just act is in question
— compulsion itself loses much of its bitter quality—for
my part"—I de—yes—I do—give up—for ever—my
sweet dear little charming ungrateful Iscagli.

Alkm.　The purest incense shall be offered up for
your prosperity, the fervent vows of two guileless
hearts.　Yes, my Iscagli, even amid that annihila-
tion of earthly cares, that oblivious bliss which crowns
successful love, we will stoop to earth.　We will
fetter the happy soul with one care; it shall be for
the Welfare of our Benefactors.

F　I　N　A　L　E.

Iscagli.

Who in absence long have known
What it is to sigh alone,
As they sit and faintly trace
Features of a favour'd race.

Leonora *and* Julia.

What in sad vicissitude
Idle hopes and doubts to brood,
Melting now at faith approv'd,
Fearing now, what once they lov'd.

Garcias.